SPORTS SUPERSTARS

LIONEL MESSI

By Anthony K. Hewson

Kaleidoscope

Minneapolis, MN

Your Front Row Seat to the Games

....

*This edition is co-published by agreement between
Kaleidoscope and World Book, Inc.*

Kaleidoscope Publishing, Inc.
6012 Blue Circle Drive
Minnetonka, MN 55343 U.S.A.

World Book, Inc.
180 North LaSalle St., Suite 900
Chicago IL 60601 U.S.A.

Kaleidoscope ISBNs
978-1-64519-042-4 (library bound)
978-1-64494-199-7 (paperback)
978-1-64519-143-8 (ebook)

World Book ISBN
978-0-7166-4346-3 (library bound)

Library of Congress Control Number
2019940061

TABLE OF
CONTENTS

Rescuing Barca

As usual, Lionel Messi made a perfect pass. He flicked the ball forward. Then he took off running.

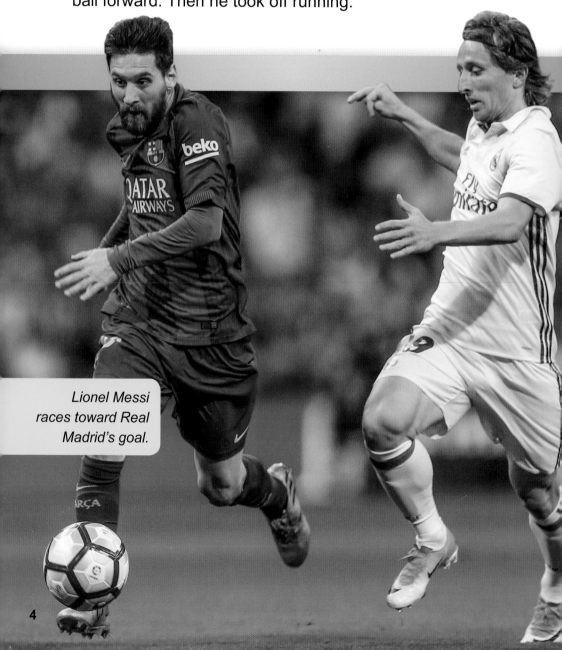

Lionel Messi races toward Real Madrid's goal.

Messi wanted to get open. He ran toward the penalty area. His Barcelona teammate saw him and rolled the ball his way. Messi got there just before a Real Madrid defender.

Messi **dribbled** into the box. A defender tried to take the ball away. But Messi moved his feet as fast as lightning. He tapped the ball to the left. It was just him and the goalkeeper. Messi fired the ball into the net. Goal! The match was tied 1–1.

FUN FACT

Barcelona and Real Madrid have been playing against each other since 1902.

This was *El Clasico*, a match between Real Madrid and Barcelona. Barcelona is also known as Barca. Few **rivalries** anywhere are as fierce. And this 2017 game was extra important. First place in the Spanish league was on the line.

As usual, it was a tight game. Barcelona took a 2–1 lead in the 73rd minute. But Real tied it in the 85th. Time was running out.

Soon Messi found his opportunity. He ran up the field. Teammate Jordi Alba was out wide with the ball. The two had played together for years. Messi knew just where to go.

FUN FACT
Messi is the all-time *El Clasico* leader in goals and assists.

Messi shoots and scores against Real Madrid.

Messi had much to celebrate in Barcelona's win over Real Madrid.

Alba headed to the top of the box. Messi found an open space. Then Alba found Messi. The ball rolled perfectly to the star forward. He struck it with his left foot. The keeper reached. But it was too far. Goal! Barcelona went on to win 3–2. The crowd in Madrid was stunned.

Messi pulled his jersey off and held it up. He wanted fans to look at his name and number. They wouldn't forget who just beat them. Barcelona was now tied with Real atop the standings. And Messi's second goal was extra sweet. It was his 500th for the club.

RECORD SCORER

Of all Messi's incredible years, 2012 might have been the best. He scored 91 goals in 69 games. That was an all-time record. He scored 79 for Barcelona. Twelve were for the Argentina national team.

CHAPTER 2

The Old Boy

The boy slides in and takes the ball away. In an instant, he is up and dribbling. He moves around defenders like they're standing still. The ball looks like it's on a string tied to his foot. He easily scores a goal. Even as a boy, Lionel Messi dazzled all who watched him.

Lionel was born on June 24, 1987. Friends called him Leo. He grew up in Rosario, Argentina. At age six, he joined the **academy** for a local soccer team. It was called Newell's Old Boys. Leo scored four goals in his first match. He teammates were good, too. In four years together, they lost only one game. But of the great young players, Leo stood out the most.

The Newell's Old Boys academy is in Rosario, Argentina.

FUN FACT

Lionel has said he wants to one day play for the Newell's Old Boys senior team.

Stories began to spread about his talent. In six seasons with Newell's, Leo was said to have scored 500 goals. Could he really have scored that many?

"At least," his coach, Adrian Coria, said. However, officially he scored 234 goals.

Something wasn't right. Leo was always a small kid. Now he was nine. But he simply wasn't growing. The team sent him to see a doctor. The doctor said Leo needed daily shots of medicine. They would help him grow. But Leo was worried. Tears ran down his face.

Diego Maradona led Argentina to the 1986 World Cup title.

"Will I grow?" he asked the doctor.

"You will be taller than Maradona," he replied.

Maradona had been a superstar. He led Argentina to the 1986 World Cup title. And he stood only 5-foot-5 (1.65 m). Height was never a problem for him.

FUN FACT

In 2010, Diego Maradona coached Lionel and the Argentina national team at the World Cup.

Where Messi Has Been

1 **Rosario, Argentina:** Messi's hometown.

2 **Barcelona, Spain:** Messi moved to this Spanish city at age 13 to play for FC Barcelona.

3 **Porto, Portugal:** Messi made his Barcelona first-team debut as a 16-year-old here in 2003.

4 **Budapest, Hungary:** Messi made his first-team debut for Argentina here in 2005.

5 **Paris, France:** Messi won his first Champions League title with Barcelona here in 2006.

6 **Beijing, China:** Messi won an Olympic gold medal with Argentina here in 2008.

7 **Rio de Janeiro, Brazil:** Messi and Argentina finished second at the 2014 FIFA World Cup here.

The shots were expensive. Newell's soon couldn't afford to pay for them. Neither could Leo's family. Then they got a call. FC Barcelona loved Leo's talent. The Spanish club offered to pay for his treatment. Leo was just 13. But he and his dad moved to Spain. He was **homesick**. He hid from his dad when he had to cry. But the doctor was right. Leo grew to 5-foot-7 (1.7 m). And he played with skill beyond his years.

Young Lionel found a home at Barcelona.

CHAPTER 3

Leo

Messi goes tearing up the field. He passes the ball. It comes right back. He hammers home a goal into the top netting.

Usually when Messi scores he points up to the sky. He does that to honor his grandmother. But today Messi has another celebration. It is June 2, 2012. Argentina is beating Ecuador. And Messi grabs the ball. He places it under the front of his shirt. This is a signal to his girlfriend, Antonella Roccuzzo. She is watching from home. The celebration is also an announcement. Roccuzzo is due with the couple's first son.

FUN FACT
Childhood friends, Messi and Roccuzzo began dating around 2007 and married in 2017.

Messi races up the field against Ecuador in 2012.

Messi poses for a picture with his wife, Antonella Roccuzzo, and their son Thiago.

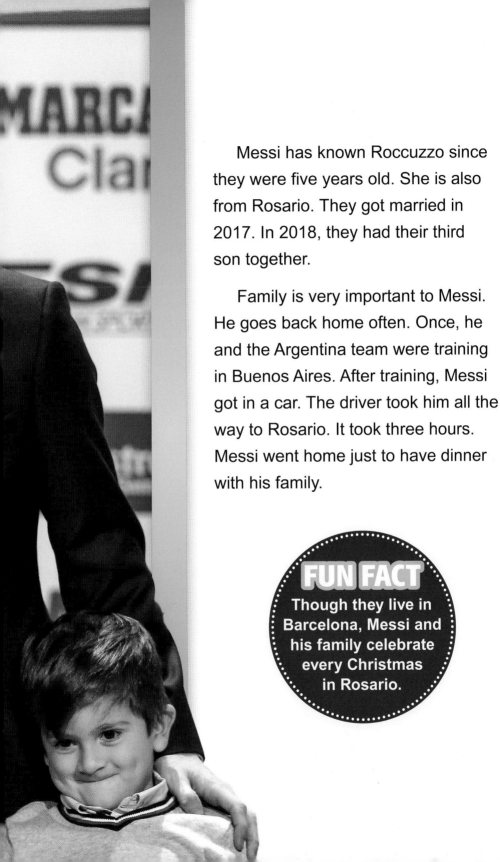

Messi has known Roccuzzo since they were five years old. She is also from Rosario. They got married in 2017. In 2018, they had their third son together.

Family is very important to Messi. He goes back home often. Once, he and the Argentina team were training in Buenos Aires. After training, Messi got in a car. The driver took him all the way to Rosario. It took three hours. Messi went home just to have dinner with his family.

FUN FACT

Though they live in Barcelona, Messi and his family celebrate every Christmas in Rosario.

Messi takes care of his hometown. He paid for soccer fields and equipment for kids. He donated money to build living spaces for Newell's Old Boys players.

Messi helps people around the world, too. He works with two major **charities**. One is the United Nations Children's Fund (UNICEF). Messi promotes the organization, which helps children around the world. Messi also has his own charity. The Leo Messi Foundation helps fund health care for children. Messi cares a lot about the cause because of his own childhood health condition.

Messi speaks with students as part of his work with UNICEF.

CAREER TIMELINE

1987

June 24, 1987
Messi is born in Rosario, Argentina.

1994
Messi begins playing with Newell's Old Boys.

1994

2001

2001
Messi signs with Barcelona and moves to Spain.

November 16, 2003
Messi makes his first-team debut with Barcelona.

2003

2008

August 23, 2008
Messi wins an Olympic gold medal with Argentina in Beijing, China.

2009
Messi wins his first World Player of the Year Award.

2009

2012

2012
Messi sets a record for most goals in a calendar year with 91.

July 13, 2014
Messi leads Argentina to the World Cup final, but the team loses to Germany.

2014

2016

2016
Messi retires from the national team, but he later changes his mind.

March 4, 2018
Messi scores his 600th career goal as Barcelona beats Atletico Madrid.

2018

CHAPTER 4

World's Best

Messi slowly drifts forward. The defender looks away. That gives Messi just enough time. He sneaks behind the Germany defense. Lucas Biglia sends him a perfect pass. Now it's just Messi and the goalie.

Messi takes on a German defender in the 2014 World Cup final.

Messi had been in this position many times. Never had the stakes been this high. Argentina was in the 2014 World Cup final. A win would make them world champions. With his left foot, Messi shot the ball. The ball got past the goalie. But it sailed just wide of the goal.

FUN FACT

Messi won the Golden Ball as the best player at the 2014 World Cup.

Messi doesn't miss often. He has led Barcelona to many championships. But success with Argentina has been harder to find. His shot was one of the team's best chances. But it was not enough. Germany won 1–0.

Messi and Argentina gave their all but fell short of the 2014 World Cup.

Losing this game was hard on Messi. The people of Argentina were eager for a victory. Messi gave it his all. He was fantastic throughout the tournament. But the team fell just short.

OLYMPIC GOLD

Argentina did win one major tournament with Messi. He was named to the 2008 Olympic team. Messi led Argentina to the gold medal. He set up the game-winning goal.

Still, fans knew of Messi's ability. No one doubted his skill. With Barcelona, he was a huge star. The team played a unique style of soccer. It was fun to watch. And it helped the team win a lot of games. On April 29, 2018, Messi scored a **hat trick**. This one was special. Barcelona won the game and its 25th league title.

The same week, Messi was named team captain for the following year. He was a team leader. But he had never been captain before. It was a symbol of all he meant to Barcelona. Everyone knew he was a great player. But he was also a great person and leader of the club.

FUN FACT

Messi has won the Ballon d'Or as the world's best player five times. Only Cristiano Ronaldo has won as many.

Barcelona fans have much to cheer for when Messi is on the field.

CAREER
STATS

CLUB APPEARANCES	**687**
CLUB GOALS	**603**
INTERNATIONAL APPEARANCES	**130**
INTERNATIONAL GOALS	**67**

BEYOND
THE BOOK

After reading the book, it's time to think about what you learned. Try the following exercises to jumpstart your ideas.

THINK

THAT'S NEWS TO ME. Chapter Four talks about Messi playing in the 2014 World Cup final. What news sources would have covered this event? What additional info might these sources have about the game? Where would you find these sources?

CREATE

PRIMARY SOURCES. A primary source is a source that contains firsthand information. That means it comes directly from the people who lived through the event. What are some primary sources that would have info on Messi? Create a list of some ideas.

SHARE

SUM IT UP. Write a paragraph that summarizes this entire book. Be sure to use your own words; don't recycle any text from the book. Share your paragraph with a classmate. What did your classmate think? Was there any feedback? Did he or she have any questions?

GROW

REAL-LIFE RESEARCH. You can learn a lot about Messi by reading about him. But what places could you visit to learn more about him? What would you experience there? What other topics could be explored at these places?

RESEARCH NINJA

Visit *www.ninjaresearcher.com/0424* to learn how to take your research skills and book report writing to the next level!

RESEARCH

DIGITAL LITERACY TOOLS

SEARCH LIKE A PRO
Learn about how to use search engines to find useful websites.

FACT OR FAKE?
Discover how you can tell a trusted website from an untrustworthy resource.

TEXT DETECTIVE
Explore how to zero in on the information you need most.

SHOW YOUR WORK
Research responsibly— learn how to cite sources.

WRITE

GET TO THE POINT
Learn how to express your main ideas.

PLAN OF ATTACK
Learn prewriting exercises and create an outline.

DOWNLOADABLE REPORT FORMS

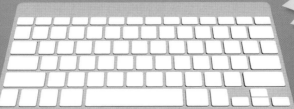

Further Resources

BOOKS

Fishman, Jon M. *Soccer Superstar Lionel Messi*. Lerner Publications, 2020.

Logothetis, Paul. *Lionel Messi*. Abdo Publishing, 2016.

Savage, Jeff. *FC Barcelona: Soccer Champions*. Lerner Publications, 2018.

WEBSITES

FACTSURFER

Factsurfer.com gives you a safe, fun way to find more information.

1. Go to www.factsurfer.com.

2. Enter "Lionel Messi" into the search box and click 🔍.

3. Select your book cover to see a list of related websites.

Glossary

academy: An academy is a place where people go to learn. Messi joined the Newell's Old Boys academy.

charities: Charities are organizations that provide money or supplies to people in need. Messi works with several charities.

dribbled: When players tap the ball between their feet to keep it moving and keep it away from defenders, they are said to have dribbled the ball. Messi dribbled between two defenders.

hat trick: A player scores a hat trick when he or she records three or more goals in a single game. Messi scored a hat trick for Barcelona.

homesick: People who miss their home are homesick. Messi was homesick for Argentina when he first moved to Barcelona.

rivalries: Rivalries are strong competitive feelings that certain athletes or teams feel when playing each other. Barcelona and Real Madrid have one of the fiercest rivalries in world sports.

Index

PHOTO CREDITS

The images in this book are reproduced through the courtesy of: Pro Shots Photo Agency/ Sipa USA/AP Images, front cover (center); Andrea Comas/AP Images, front cover (right), p. 3; Krivosheev Vitaly/Shutterstock Images, front cover (background); Francisco Seco/AP Images, pp. 4, 6–7; charnsitr/Shutterstock Images, p. 5; Alterphotos/Sipa/AP Images, p. 8; Natacha Pisarenko/AP Images, pp. 9–10, 16–17; Carlo Fumagalli/AP Images, p. 12; AGIF/Shutterstock Images, p. 13; Red Line Editorial, pp. 14, 21 (timeline); Peter Schneider/Keystone/AP Images, p. 15; Manu Fernandez/AP Images, pp. 18–19, 20; Donot6_Studio/Shutterstock, pp. 21 (ball), 30; Hassan Ammar/AP Images, pp. 22–23; Frank Augstein/AP Images, p. 24; Luca Bruno/ AP Images, p. 25; Sergio Ros de Mora/Imaginechina/AP Images, p. 26; Ververidis Vasilis/ Shutterstock, p. 27.

ABOUT THE AUTHOR

Anthony K. Hewson is a freelance writer originally from San Diego, now living in the Bay Area with his wife and their two dogs.